SCOTLAND
in the time of
BURNS

First published in Great Britain
in Merlins in 1996

HB ISBN 0 86241 638 8

PB ISBN 0 86241 654 X

Cataloguing-in-Publication Data
*A catalogue record for this title is
available upon request from the British
Library*

The publisher acknowledges subsidy from the Scottish Arts Council
towards publication of this volume

Typeset and designed by
Artisan Graphics, Edinburgh

Printed and bound by
Oriental Press, Dubai

CANONGATE BOOKS LTD
14 HIGH STREET EDINBURGH EH1 1TE

SCOTLAND

In the time of Burns

Iain Rose & Donald Gunn

CANONGATE • MERLINS

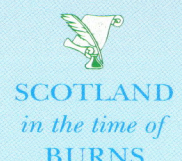

SCOTLAND
in the time of
BURNS

Contents

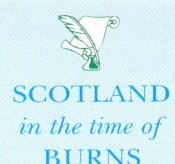

— 1 —

Learning and Language

On 25 January 1759, Robert Burns was born into a poor, farming family in a small cottage in Alloway, near Ayr. He became the most famous Scot ever, and one of the world's best-loved poets and songwriters.

People in Scotland and much of the world celebrate his birthday with Burns Suppers. They enjoy a traditional Scottish meal and remember his life and work with speeches, poems and songs.

When some of his poems were published in 1786, an important novelist called Henry MacKenzie praised Burns as a "heaven-taught ploughman from his humble and unlettered station" (uneducated position in life).

This helped to build the myth of Burns as a simple peasant. Burns cleverly encouraged this idea about himself because it drew attention to his poems.

The truth was different. Robert's father, William, and his neighbours had shared the cost of hiring a teacher for their children. Arrangements like this were common at the time because many parts of Scotland had no proper schools. Robert's lessons included the Bible, the works of Scottish and English writers, arithmetic and English grammar. He was a brilliant pupil. Lowland Scots are

The cottage in Alloway where Burns was born.

Burns called this portrait by Alexander Reid, "By far the best likeness of me ever taken."

At Burns Suppers, a haggis is cut open as these lines are spoken.

From To A HAGGIS

His knife see rustic Labour[1] dight[2],
An cut you up wi ready slight[3],
Trenching your gushing entrails bright,
  Like onie[4] ditch;
And then, O what a glorious sight,
  Warm-reekin, rich!

1 country worker
2 wipe
3 skill
4 any

proud that Burns wrote in their own language, Scots. His first book described his poems as being "chiefly in the Scottish dialect". But Burns also wrote in English.

Scots had been the language of the Scottish Kings and government. English was slowly replacing it and, by Burns's time, most serious writers wrote in English. However, nearly all Lowlanders could still speak Scots.

Burns was able to use English or Scots and even to mix them as it suited him in his busy life as a writer and hard-working farmer.

SCOTS: WHAT'S IN A NAME?

Over the years the languages spoken in Scotland have changed. So have their names.

The Scots came from Ireland and spoke Gaelic.

➡ *Gaelic spread throughout Scotland.*

➡ *Some people in South East Scotland and North East England spoke Inglis (a northern kind of English).*

➡ *These Inglis speakers called the Gaelic language 'Scottis' (Scots).*

➡ *Slowly, Inglis replaced Gaelic in most of Lowland Scotland.*

➡ *After that, some Lowlanders began to call their Inglis language by the name 'Scottis' and to call the original Scottish language 'Erse' (Irish).*

➡ *Nowadays the original Scottish language is called Gaelic. Inglis is known as 'Scots' or 'The Doric'.*

— 2 —

Agricultural Revolution

For most of his life Robert Burns lived and worked on a farm. This was a time when the way of farming in the Lowlands of Scotland changed so much that it was called the 'Agricultural Revolution'.

Landowners wanted their land 'improved'. They wanted their farmers to dig drains and to mix lime with the earth to make it better for crops. They also wanted farmers to protect their fields from the wind by building 'dry-stane' dykes or growing hedges and by planting groups of trees to form 'wind breaks'.

Landowners hoped that better farms would produce bigger harvests so the farmers could earn more money and pay them bigger rents.

These improvements, however, were expensive and they took years of hard work. Farmers did not have machines to help them. All the work had to be done by hand.

The landowners helped the farmers by offering them money to pay for improvements and by giving them low rents for the first few years after they agreed to make improvements.

Building a dry-stane dyke is skilled and hard work.

William Burns became the tenant of Lochlea farm in Ayrshire. He planned to improve it.

Improvements were not always successful. When he was seven years old, Robert's family moved to the farm at Mount Oliphant, near Ayr. Many years later, Robert's brother, Gilbert, wrote that the land there was "almost the poorest soil I know of in a state of cultivation...We lived very sparingly. For several years butcher's meat was a stranger to the house."

The family found it very difficult to make enough money to pay the rent.

The family's problems increased when their landowner died and a cruel factor began to collect the rent. Afterwards, Burns wrote, "My indignation yet boils over at the recollection of the scoundrel tyrant's insolent, threatening letters, which used to set us all in tears."

This was an improved farm. You can see the walls which were built around it.

Burns's father, William, and his family worked very hard for eleven years to try to be successful farmers at Mount Oliphant. They then moved to a farm at Lochlea where they had to work just as hard.

The strain of all the hard work and worry caused the early death of William Burns. Robert Burns's health was also affected by too much hard work and a bad diet when he was young.

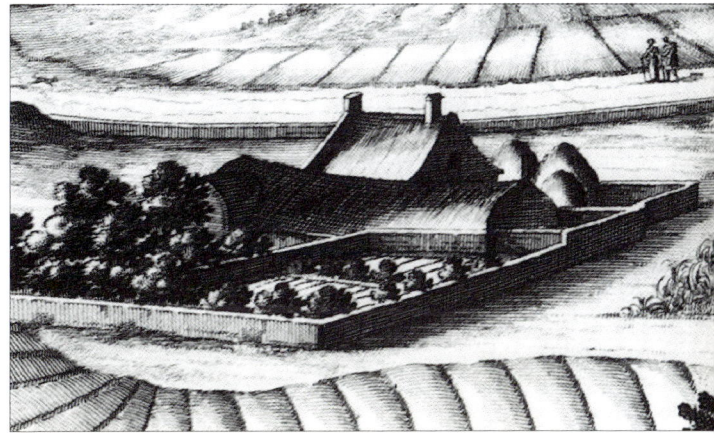

— 3 —

Daily Work

Farming, at this time, was very hard work, even on land which had been improved.

In the spring, Burns had to plough fields and to prepare them for sowing seeds. He used a horse drawn plough but this was skilled and difficult work. Burns was proud that he could plough twice as fast as an ordinary ploughman. Then he had to level the ground by using a horse drawn harrow before he could sow his seeds.

Burns used the broadcast method for sowing. He carried the seeds in a bag or basket and walked across the fields scattering handfuls of seed across the ground. He had to be careful that the seeds were spread evenly and that he did not leave bare patches. Birds, unfortunately, ate many of the seeds sown this way.

Harvesting was especially hard work. Crops were cut by hand using scythes and sickles and then they had to be gathered by hand and carefully dried. After that, the grain had to be separated from the stalks. This was done by using a flail to hit the stalks so hard that the grains and chaff around them all fell off.

From **TO A MOUSE**

In this poem Burns speaks to a mouse whose nest he has destroyed with his plough. The poem may have a second meaning. The comfortable life of many farmers had been destroyed by the Agricultural Revolution. In addition landowners had given farmers a lot of trouble. Burns was not going to add to the mouse's troubles by chasing it.

Wee sleekit[1], cow'rin, tim'rous beastie'
O, what a panic's in thy breastie!
Thou need na start awa sae hasty,
**   Wi bickering[2] brattle[3]!**
I wad be laith[4] to rin an chase thee,
**   Wi murdering pattle[5]!...**

That wee bit heap o leaves an stibble,
Has cost thee monie a weary nibble,
Now thou's turn'd out, for a thy trouble
**   But[6] house or hald[7],**
To thole[8] the winter's sleety dribble
**   An cranreuch[9] cauld!**

But Mousie, thou art no thy lane[10].
In proving foresight may be vain:
The best-laid schemes o mice an men
**   Gang aft agley[11],**
An lea'e us nought but grief an pain,
**   For promis'd joy!**

Still thou art blest, compar'd wi me!
The present only toucheth thee:
But och! I backward cast my e'e
**   On prospects drear[12]!**
An forward, tho I canna see,
**   I guess an fear!**

1 glossy coated or sly
2 rushing or scurrying
3 clatter or noise
4 unwilling
5 plough scraper
6 without

7 possessions
8 put up with
9 hoar-frost
10 alone
11 often go wrong
12 dreary

Finally, the grains had to be separated from the chaff by winnowing. On a windy day, the grain and chaff were tossed in the air. The light chaff blew away while the heavy grains fell to the ground where they were collected. Ordinary farmers expected to harvest three sacks of grain for every sack of seed sown in spring. Farms which had been improved expected to do far better than this, especially where farmers used 'crop rotation'.

Farmers had discovered that they would have better harvests, if they planted a different crop in each field, every year. They saw the greatest improvement when they planted a root crop, like turnips or potatoes, one year and a grain crop, like wheat or oats, the next year.

This did not always happen. After his father died Robert Burns and his brother, Gilbert, rented the farm at Mossgiel. They had very bad crops one year because they had sown bad seed. Bad weather ruined their harvest the next year.

Farm animals also improved during the Agricultural Revolution. They were given better grazing in 'enclosed fields', They were fed turnips during the winter. Farmers kept their best animals for breeding and this was how special breeds of sheep and cattle, like the Aberdeen Angus, or the 'Highland Cow' appeared. When he had his last farm at Ellisland, in Dumfries-shire, Robert Burns gave up growing crops and kept a herd of Galloway cows instead. These cows became famous for producing milk.

For many landowners the Agricultural Revolution was a great success. Their farms were worth more and they collected bigger rents. For most farmers it involved hard work for many years and their effort did not always benefit them.

All the farm work had to be done by hand.

— 4 —

Bogles
and
Bibles

After the day's work, families often gathered together. Depending on their backgrounds and their religious beliefs, they might share anything from tales of the supernatural and folk songs to Bible readings and psalm singing.

While he was growing up, Robert Burns, like many other young Scots, enjoyed a mixture of both these customs. Robert's mother had a fine voice and sang old, Scottish airs and ballads. From her, he learned the love of his country's folk music which later inspired him to write, collect or improve hundreds of Scottish songs.

Betty Davidson, an elderly relative, filled his head with superstitious stories about fairies, bogles and witches. The poem 'Tam o' Shanter' was based on a local witch tale.

In the Highlands, such tales were very common as were songs of every kind and adventure stories about warrior heroes from history and legend.

An evening in a Scots cottage - music and story telling.

The witch chases Tam o' Shanter and his mare, Meg.

'The Cottar's Saturday Night' by David Allen. Burns's head was used as a model for the eldest son sitting next to his father – and there is a child snipping off the cat's tail with scissors!

Although most schooling in Scotland was based on written English, people passed on the country's folk traditions by word of mouth in Scots or in Gaelic, The minds of many of the ordinary people were like treasure chests full of Scotland's music and memories, but not everyone placed a high value on such things. Some sternly religious people saw them as a silly waste of time, or even sinful!

It was common for religious fathers to lead their families in bible-reading, psalm singing and prayer. This was William Burns's habit. Every night he, his wife and their seven children would gather together for family worship. This made a deep impression on Robert. His poem, 'The Cottar's Saturday Night' paints an affectionate picture of a typical Christian family gathering.

A wealthy friend was thrilled with the poem, but her old servant could not see anything remarkable about it. "Nae doubt gentlemen and ladies think muckle o't," she said, "but for me it's naething but what I saw in my ain faither's house every night and I dinna see how he could hae tauld it any other way."

From **THE COTTAR'S SATURDAY NIGHT.**

*The chearfu supper done, wi serious face,
They, round the ingle [1], form a circle wide;
The sire turns o'er, wi patriarchal [2] grace,
The big Ha-Bible [3], ance [4] his father's pride.
His bonnet rev'rently is laid aside,
His lyart haffets [5] wearing thin and bare;
Those strains [6] that once did sweet in Zion [7] glide,
He wales [8] a portion with judicious [9] care;
And 'Let us worship God!' he says with solemn air.*

1 fireplace
2 fatherly
3 Hall Bible
4 once
5 grey side-whiskers
6 melodies
7 the Holy Land
8 chooses
9 wise

When Burns was a young man the government wanted farmers to grow flax. Its seeds were used to make linseed oil and oil-cake which could be fed to cattle. The stalks were used for making linen, but it was a slow and difficult process.

In fact, the government paid farmers extra money to grow this crop. In 1783, Robert Burns received three pounds for growing flax. This was about half-a-year's wages for a farm worker.

Flax grew to about a half-a-metre in height. When it was fully grown, each stalk had to be pulled, by hand, out of the ground and left to dry. The seeds were separated from the stalk and then these stalks of flax had to be 'dressed'.

They were put into a 'lint-hole' until the woody part of the stalk had rotted. Then the fibres had to be separated from the rotten wood. This was done by hitting the stalks with a small hammer to break and knock off the woody bits (scutching) and then by combing the fibres to clean them (heckling).

The flax dresser wanted long strands of fibre which he would 'card' by using two brushes to turn it into a light fluffy mass called 'line'. Women called 'spinsters' could then turn this into linen thread at home on their spinning wheels. Weavers would then weave this thread into cloth.

This drawing from 1783 shows the breaking and scutching of flax in a mill. This is part of the process of preparing the flax for weaving.

These two poems were written when Burns was in Irvine and his business as a flax-dresser failed.

RAGING FORTUNE

O, raging Fortune's withering blast
Has laid my leaf full low!
O, raging Fortune's withering blast
Has laid my leaf full low.

My stem was fair, my bud was green,
My blossom sweet did blow;
The dew fell fresh, the sun rose mild,
And made my branches grow.

But luckless Fortune's northern storms
Laid a' my blossoms low!
But luckless Fortune's northern storms
Laid a' my blossoms low!

I'LL GO AND BE A SODGER[1]

O, why the deuce[2] should I repine[3],
And be an ill foreboder[4]?
I'm twenty three, and five feet nine,
I'll go and be a sodger!

I gat some gear[5] wi meikle[6] care,
I held it weel thegither[7];
But now it's gane[8] – and something mair[9]:
I'll go and be a sodger!

1 soldier
2 why on earth
3 be sorry
4 a person who expects the worst
5 wealth
6 much
7 together
8 gone
9 more

Usually, about half of the fibres were lost during this process. The stalks might be too short, or they might become so tangled and knotted that they were useless for weaving. The waste could only be used for padding and for packaging and so it was worth very little. An unskilled flax dresser could waste even more of the flax.

After growing his crop of flax in 1781, Robert Burns went to Irvine to learn how to be a flax dresser. He hoped to do that instead of being a farmer. He used all his hard-earned money to buy a share in a heckling mill and found lodgings in the town.

Irvine, where Burns worked as a flax dresser.

But, everything went wrong. He disliked the work. He became ill. He was cheated by his business partner. Finally, on New Year's Day 1782, the mill caught fire and Burns was left without even a sixpence! He wrote a number of very gloomy poems about ruin and death but, on a lighter note, he wrote about going away to be a soldier. This was what many poor, young men did at that time. In fact, Burns went home to his father's farm at Lochlea.

Besides, the linen trade in Scotland was soon overtaken by the spectacular growth of the cotton trade.

Mills

Scotland was beginning to industrialise during Burns's lifetime. In many trades, water and steam-powered machinery in factories was taking over from making things by hand at home. The old 'Domestic System' was being replaced by the new 'Factory System'.

The textile trade, which produced cloth, was one of the first to industrialise. Spinsters lost their jobs when new machines like the 'Spinning Jenny', the 'Water Frame' and the 'Mule' were invented to spin thread.

These inventions could spin much faster than a woman at home with her spinning wheel. After that, nobody bought expensive, hand-spun thread from spinsters.

The new machines were too big to fit into a spinster's cottage, too expensive for them to buy and needed a water-wheel to drive them. Rich men built factories, housing many machines, beside fast-flowing rivers. The spinsters had to go there to work.

Often, these new factories were in out-of-the-way places like Catrine or the Falls of Clyde. New villages and towns had to be built to house their workers. In 1785, to attract workers to his mills at New Lanark, David Dale offered them homes as well as jobs. Within ten years he had 1,157 people working there.

More than 800 of these workers were children. Most employers preferred children to adults because their small, nimble fingers could handle the threads easily.

These new machines were especially good for spinning cotton. It was becoming more popular than wool or linen for clothes.

Cotton was a light material which could be washed easily and look as good as new after being washed. It was also cheaper than linen or wool.

All the thread from these new mills had to be turned into cloth, so weavers were in great demand. Weaving was still done at home at this time because no satisfactory machine had been invented for weaving. It was usually a man's job and many men wanted to become 'wabsters'. They earned more money than most other workers and they only had to work four days a week!

This picture of a spinster at her spinning wheel was taken late in the nineteenth century, but the process had not changed much since the days of Burns

Cotton mill were noisy, dusty places. The workers, who were often children, had to keep up with the speed of the machines.

Weavers were envied by many workers because they had so much free time and spare money. They used it to play sports and to argue about politics and religion.

The amount of linen manufactured in Scotland doubled during Burns's lifetime. The amount of cotton increased thirty times. As factories, industries and the towns beside them grew, Burns saw Scotland was changing in front of his eyes.

Burns imagines himself married to a spinster. He pokes fun at her for being so slow.

From THE WEARY PUND[1] O TOW[2]

I bought my wife a stane[3] o lint[4]
As guid[5] as e'er did grow,
And a' that she has made o that
Is ae[6] puir[7] pund o tow.

Chorus
The weary pund, the weary pund,
The weary pund o tow!
I think my wife will end her life
Before she spin her tow.

1 pound (0.4kg.)	4 partly-dressed flax
2 linen threads	5 good
3 stone (5kg.)	6 one
	7 poor

Weaving on a hand-loom in a cottage. The woman on the right is using a wheel to spin the yarn.

Heavy Industry

In the late 18th century, heavy industries, like coal mining and iron making, were beginning to grow in the Central Belt of Scotland between Glasgow and Edinburgh.

Townsfolk used coal for cooking and to heat their homes. More coal was needed as the towns and cities grew bigger. Farmers needed coal to burn limestone to make the lime which they needed to improve their fields. The iron industry also began to use coal to make iron.

Mine owners produced more coal by employing more workers, making their mines deeper and bigger, and by opening up new coal mines. Mining towns and villages were growing because unemployed farm-workers, Highlanders and Irishmen went there looking for work.

However, the terrible working conditions in the mines frightened some men away. Besides, many people looked down on miners. They knew that criminals who had been sentenced to death were given the choice of hanging or working in coal mines. Until 1799 miners were 'astricted', which meant that the children of miners had to become miners.

The Scottish iron industry began to grow after Abraham Darby discovered how to use coke to smelt iron ore. Coke is made from coal. In Scotland coal and iron ore were often found very close to each other.

Samuel Garbett, John Roebuck and William Cadell decided to build their iron works at Carron because it was close to coal and iron ore. It was also close to the River Forth so they could move goods cheaply by boat.

After the Forth and Clyde Canal was dug this became even easier.

The top picture shows how cooking once had to be done on an open fire. The bottom one shows the advantages of the Carron range

Ironworks caused pollution with their fumes. In this picture of Falkirk in 1824 you can see the smoke belching out from Carron Ironworks. The heat and flames from the furnaces made Burns think of Hell.

He went to visit the Carron Ironworks in 1787 but he went on a Saturday and the gatekeeper would not let him in!

In a bad temper, Burns immediately made up this poem.

ON CARRON WORKS

We cam na here to see your warks
In hopes to be mair wise,
But only, lest we gang to Hell,
It may be nae surprise.

But when we tirl'd[1] at your door
Your porter dought na bear us[2]:
Sae may, should we to Hell's yetts[3]
come
Your billy[4] Satan sair[5] us.

1 rattled at the door by turning the latch
2 did not dare to let us in
3 gates
4 fellow
5 serve

Carron was the first 'integrated' ironworks where all the work was done at one place. Coal was brought there and turned into coke. Iron ore was smelted, and finished iron goods like nails and spades were produced. Carron was most famous for its heavy guns called 'Carronades' which were used by the Royal Navy and the British Army.

In Scotland Carron was well known for its kitchen ranges. Every housewife wanted one, even if they were expensive. When Robert Burns built his new house at Ellisland in 1789, he bought a Carron range for his wife, Jean Armour.

A Carronade.

— 8 —

Transport

Scotland was changing because of the Agricultural and Industrial Revolutions. Farmers, businessmen and even ordinary workers moved about the countryside far more than they had in the past because they had to transport materials like coal and iron as well as finished goods like cloth and machinery.

Farmers, for example, had to take coal and limestone to their farms so they could prepare lime to improve the soil. This meant that roads had to be improved.

The government had already made new, military roads to connect the forts it had built in the Highlands. These roads made it easier for the government to move men and supplies into the areas which had supported the Jacobite Risings.

THE TWO BRIDGES AT AYR
painted by Henry Duguid

In the Lowlands, the government allowed groups of important people to take over and improve the main roads in their own areas. There groups were called 'Turnpike Trusts'. They were allowed to charge road users 'tolls' at barriers called 'turnpikes' which were placed across the roads at toll houses.

The Turnpike Trusts used their toll money to pay for road improvements. Very often, the Turnpike Trust had to build completely new roads because the old ones were just dirt tracks. They also spent money building bridges.

The new roads and bridges made it easier to travel across Scotland. Rich people travelled in horsedrawn coaches. Most travellers still went on horseback.

In flatter parts of the country, waterways called canals were dug. This was because it was easier and cheaper to move heavy goods by boat.

The Royal Mail service improved along with the transport system. New Post Offices opened in more towns across Scotland and mail services became more regular. At that time, however, stamps had not been invented and the person receiving the letter had to pay for its delivery.

Burns was a great letter writer. He also received letters from all over Scotland although he must have found it difficult to pay for their delivery. Many of these letters have been preserved and published in books.

Two road engineers were famous for building roads.

Telford's roads had strong stone foundations. They were expensive to build but cheap to maintain.

MacAdam's roads did not have such expensive foundations. They were cheap to build but they were more expensive to keep in good order.

From THE BRIGS¹ OF AYR

Burns imagines the old bridge (built in 1232) and the new bridge (built 1788) having an argument about which was best.

The New Bridge says to the old one

Auld Vandal! ye but show your little mense²,
Just much about it wi your scanty sense:
Will your poor, narrow foot-path of a street,
Where two wheel-barrows tremble when they meet,
Your ruin'd, formless bulk o stane and lime,
Compare wi bonnie brigs o modern time?

The Old Bridge replies to the new one

Conceited gowk³! puffed up wi windy pride!
This monie⁴ a year I've stood the flood an tide;
And tho wi crazy eild⁵ I'm sair forfair⁶.
I'll be a brig where ye're a shapeless cairn!

1 bridge
2 good manners
3 cuckoo
4 many
5 old age
6 completely worn

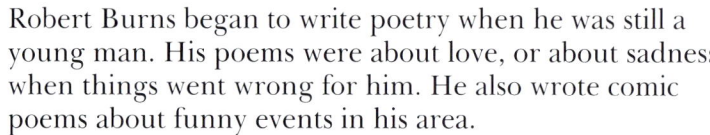

Robert Burns began to write poetry when he was still a young man. His poems were about love, or about sadness when things went wrong for him. He also wrote comic poems about funny events in his area.

Paper was expensive and Robert had to write his poems by hand, using a quill pen and ink. His friends found out about his talent and they began to ask him for copies. Gradually, Burns became well known in his area for writing good poems. Eventually, they suggested that he should publish them.

This was going to cost Burns a lot of money. He would have to pay for the paper and the printers' time in setting up the type. At that time all the letters and punctuation marks were on separate blocks. Each one had to be put in place very carefully and this took time and was expensive. Burns would have to check each page very carefully to make sure that there were no mistakes. Finally, he would have to pay for its covers and to employ men to bind the pages into a book.

Burns decided to print a 'subscription issue'. People would be asked to promise to buy the book and, if he had enough promises to pay all the bills, then he would print it. Burns hoped to sell some extra copies to make some money for himself. In fact, he hoped to earn enough money to go to Jamaica, He planned to marry, and to start a new life there with Margaret Campbell whom he called 'Highland Mary'.

His collection of poems "chiefly in the Scottish dialect", was published in Kilmarnock. It was a huge success. Some readers sent copies to their friends in Edinburgh who wrote to Burns and praised him as a poet. They wanted him to go to Edinburgh to print his poems there.

Burns wrote his poetry using a quill pen, which was a feather cut at the tip to form a nib. He would use a solid block of ink and sand for blotting. Some people had all these in a writing set like this one.

To print a book every letter had to be put in place by hand. Once all the letters for the pages had been put together, sheets of paper were put into the press one at a time. Producing a book took a long time and needed many different skills.

Burns had a difficult choice: to go to Jamaica or to Edinburgh, where people were saying he was 'Scotland's poet'. He delayed his journey.

Margaret Campbell went to Greenock to wait for him. Unfortunately, while she was waiting, she caught typhus and died. Burns went to Edinburgh to seek fame and, he hoped, fortune.

The picture below shows the Customs House at Greenock in 1820. It also shows the sort of ships which used the busy port. On the right is a model of the statue of Highland Mary which stands at Greenock.

— 10 —

Edinburgh

Burns first visited Edinburgh in the winter of 1786, just after his poems were published in Kilmarnock, He stayed in a part of the city known as the Old Town.

Its buildings soared to ten or twelve storeys in height. People from all walks of life shared the same building, so a carpenter might meet a countess on the stairs.

The upper classes, such as professors, judges, lawyers and aristocrats lived on the middle floors. Clerks and merchants lived above and below them, while ordinary working people filled the attics and the poorest crammed the cellars.

Burns wrote this poem soon after he arrived in the city.

From ADDRESS TO EDINBURGH

Edina[1]! Scotia's darling seat[2]!
  All hail thy palaces and tow'rs
Where once, beneath a Monarch's feet,
  Sat Legislation's sovereign powers[3]....

Here Wealth still swells the golden tide,
  As busy Trade his labour plies;
There Architecture's noble pride[4]
  Bids elegance and splendour rise...

With awe-struck thought and pitying tears,
  I view that noble, stately dome,
Where Scotia's kings of other years,
  Fam'd heroes! had their royal home...

1 Edinburgh
2 capital city
3 Scotland's Parliament , abolished in 1707
4 The buildings of the New Town

Burns stayed in Baxter's Close in the Old Town of Edinburgh.

The mixing of social classes in a small area made for a colourful and lively city. Homes and work places were close together. Everyone saw everyone else and knew their business.

Unfortunately, there was no proper sewage disposal system. So people threw all kinds of filth from the windows of what were the tallest houses in Britain.

Many were content to go on living this way, but others wanted to escape from the noise, smells and lack of privacy.

For years, there was talk of building a New Town to the north of the old one.

The scheme began with the building of the first house in 1767. Gradually, the gentry moved there and found themselves living in a modern example of town planning, with streets and squares laid out in neat, regular patterns. It took until 1800 just to complete the first stage of the plan and then many more houses were added.

The Old Town was left to the poor and much of it soon became a jumble of slums. Burns rented rooms in the Old Town, but he often visited the New Town where rich and important Scots were anxious to meet 'Scotland's poet'.

This engraving of Charlotte Square shows how open and elegant Edinburgh's New Town was.

CHANGING EDINBURGH

Old Town:

How long shall the capital city of Scotland and the chief street of it stink worse than a common sewer?

— *John Wesley 1762*

New Town:

The New Town has been built upon one uniform plan, which is the only means of making a city beautiful.... In no town that I ever saw can such a contrast be found between the ancient and modern architecture.

— *Edward Topham, a visitor in 1774-75*

Old Town:

In 1763, people of quality and fashion lived in houses which in 1783 are inhabited by tradesmen and people in humble and ordinary life.

— *William Creech, Burns's publisher*

— 11 —

The Athens of the North

> J have the advice of some very wise friends among the literati here, but with them J sometimes find it necessary to claim the privilege of thinking for myself.

Letter from Burns to his friend, Mrs Dunlop, 22 March 1787.

For over sixty years Edinburgh was one of the most important centres of learning and new ideas in Europe. In 1769, an English visitor said "Here I stand at what is called the Cross of Edinburgh and can, in a few minutes, take fifty men of genius and learning by the hand."

The city was a busy hive of historians, artists, scientists, doctors, writers, engineers, architects and great thinkers. There were so many fine buildings and brilliant minds in Edinburgh that it was compared to the Ancient Greek city of Athens in its Golden Age. Scotland's capital was called 'The Athens of the North'.

There were many things of which Edinburgh felt proud, but Scottish speech was not one of them. A visitor in 1775 wrote that the wealthy people of Edinburgh were anxious "to rid themselves of a Scots accent". They even went to classes to learn to avoid 'Scotticisms' in their speech.

Burns in the home of James Burnett, Lord Monboddo.

Edinburgh's educated readers, known as the 'literati', gave Burns a hero's welcome when he first came to Edinburgh. They were fascinated by the thought that a humble farmer could write poetry so well. They thought this was simply because he lived close to Nature.

At the time many of the literati believed that Nature could inspire people in this way. A few fashionable ladies even tried to write poems in Scots, hoping to find inspiration in the language of the Lowland countryside. No wonder they were so excited by this 'Rustic Bard' or 'countryside poet'.

Burns impressed them with his personal dignity and entertained them with his clever, witty conversation. His new-found fame helped to sell more copies of his book. Burns, however, rejected advice to give up Scots and write only in English. Instead, he began his work on Scottish songs, which was his greatest achievement.

Burns's poems were published in Kilmarnock in 1786. This is the title-page of the Edinburgh Edition of Burns's poems, 1787.

In Scotland the Scots learned to write English 'as a foreign language'. Gradually, important Scots began to speak English instead of Scots or Gaelic. Lord Braxfield (1722-99), was the last Scottish judge to speak Scots during trials in his court.

THE GROWING INFLUENCE OF ENGLISH

RELIGION

English translations of the Bible were used in most Lowland Scottish homes and churches. The most famous one was the King James Authorised Version, 1611.

ROYALTY

In 1603, King James VI of Scotland became James I of England. The Scottish Royal Court left Edinburgh for London. There they had to speak English and this became the fashion among the friends of Royalty.

POLITICS

In 1707, at the Union of the Parliaments, the Scottish and English Parliaments joined together. They met in London and Scottish politicians and officials began to use English.

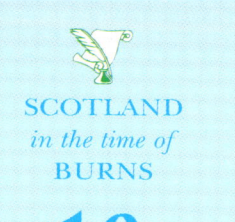
In 1787 Burns wrote to a friend that he wanted "to make leisurely pilgrimages through Caledonia; to sit on the fields of her battles; to wander on the romantic banks of her rivers; and to muse by the stately towers ... once the honoured abodes of her heroes." He was interested in the idea of becoming Scotland's poet. He wanted to see more of the country and to find fresh ideas for poems and songs.

That year, he toured the Scottish Borders, which were rich in folk songs and tales of battles. During this tour he would come upon songs like 'Sutors o Selkirk'.

Burns worked on hundreds of old songs and tunes from all over Scotland. For some songs only the choruses were remembered and most of the words had been forgotten. Others had tunes which did not fit the words properly.

Burns worked hard improving the words or writing new ones for many of these songs. He suggested better tunes for others and he wrote some completely new songs himself. These appeared in two Scottish song collections.

After his Borders tour, Burns visited the Highlands. Near Dunkeld he spent an evening with the famous fiddler Neil Gow, whose tunes are still played today.

His tour of the Highlands encouraged his work on Jacobite songs such as 'Killiecrankie', 'The Battle of Sherramuir', and 'Johnny Cope'. He visited many of the sites connected with the Jacobites, including the battlefield at Culloden on Drumossie Moor. The Jacobites were part of Scotland's recent history and, at times, Burns appeared to support them.

It's up wi the sutors o Selkirk,
And down wi the Earl o Hume;
And here is to all the braw laddies
That wear the single sol'd shoon....

This song referred to the Scottish defeat at Flodden (1513). The Selkirk sutors (shoemakers) blamed it on the Earl of Hume.

from THE LOVELY LASS O INVERNESS

Drumossie moor, Drumossie day -
A waefu[1] day it was to me!
For there I lost my father dear,
My father dear and brethren three.

Their winding-sheet[2] the bluidy clay,
Their graves are growin green to see,
And by them lies the dearest lad
That ever blest a woman's e'e[3].

1 sad
2 grave-cloth
3 eye

SCOTS WHA HAE

Burns suggested that Robert Bruce used these words to encourage his army to fight at the Battle of Bannockburn.

Scots, wha hae wi Wallace[1] bled,
Scots, wham[2] Bruce has aften led,
Welcome to your gory bed
Or to victorie!

Now's the day, and now's the hour:
See the front o battle lour[3],
See approach proud Edward's power –
Chains and slaverie!

Wha will be a traitor knave[4]?
Wha can fill a coward's grave?
Wha sae base as be a slave?
Let him turn, and flee!

Wha for Scotland's King and Law
Freedom's sword will strongly draw,
Freeman stand, or Freeman fa',
Let him follow me!

By Oppression's[5] woes and pains,
By your sons in servile[6] chains,
We will drain our dearest veins,
But they shall be free!

Lay the proud usurpers[7] low!
Tyrants[8] fall in every foe!
Liberty's in every blow! –
Let us do, or die!

Burns was particularly interested in battlefields because they stirred his imagination. He wrote this about Bannockburn where Robert Bruce defeated the English king, Edward II, in 1314.

"Here no Scot can pass uninterested. I fancy to myself that I see my gallant, heroic countrymen coming oe'r the hill, and down upon the plunderers of their country, the murderers of their fathers...the oppressive, insulting, blood-thirsty foe! I see them... exulting in their heroic, royal leader, and rescued liberty and independence!"

He used the memory of this visit to compose 'Scots Wha Hae'.

This is how an artist imagined the scene when Bruce addressed his troops at Bannockburn.

1 Sir William Wallace, an earlier leader of the Scots against the English
2 whom
3 look menacingly
4 rogue
5 cruel treatment
6 slave's
7 person who tries to take another's position
8 bullies

SCOTLAND
in the time of
BURNS

— 13 —

Highland Facts and Fantasies

MacDonell of Glengarry made a point of dressing and acting like a Highland chief.

In 1755 about one third of the Scottish population lived in the Highlands.

Lowland Scots spoke Scots and were learning to speak English. Highland Scots spoke Gaelic, the original Scottish language, and they, too, were learning to speak English.

After the Battle of Culloden in 1746, when the last Jacobite Rising was defeated, the Government banned tartan and plaids. They even banned the bagpipes and said they were 'an instrument of war'. Highlanders began to play the fiddle, just like Lowlanders.

But the two groups were still divided by their languages. Burns, like most Lowland Scots, was unaware of Gaelic culture. Indeed, he probably did not know that Duncan Ban MacIntyre, one of the greatest Gaelic poets, was composing poems at the same time, in Edinburgh, but in a different language.

The Highlands of Scotland and their history had become very popular among the educated people of Europe. This was because they thought that the Highlanders were 'noble savages' whose way of life had not been affected or spoiled by civilisation or education.

They were also fascinated by the stories of 'Bonnie Prince Charlie' and the Jacobites. They admired that fact that Highlanders had helped the Prince to escape after Culloden, even although there was a huge reward for his capture.

Indeed, many Scots whose families had not been Jacobites claimed that they had secretly helped them.

James Macpherson, a Highland scholar, took advantage of this fascination with the Highlands and ignorance of Gaelic culture to make some money for himself.

Macpherson knew the stories of ancient Gaelic heroes like Ossian and Fingal. He decided to translate them into English as poems. He told people that these were translations of ancient Gaelic poems which had been handed down by word of mouth for hundreds of years.

Many famous painters in Europe were inspired by Macpherson's poems. This one was by the French painter, Gerard.

This was not true, but nobody in Europe realised that they had been tricked. Macpherson's poems were translated into most European languages. Emperor Napoleon of France carried a copy of Macpherson's 'Ossian' wherever he went. Burns called Ossian 'the prince of Poets' and he made a special tour from Crieff to visit his grave. Artists made paintings showing these legends and musicians composed music inspired by them.

Tourists flocked to see places like Fingal's Cave on Staffa or Ossian's Cave in Glencoe. In fact, it took years for people to realise that there were no long Gaelic poems about Ossian and that Macpherson had turned these old Gaelic stories into poetry by himself.

Highland chiefs, like Alasdair MacDonell of Glengarry and MacNab of MacNab, were adding to the legends about the Highlands. They did not follow the same way of life as their ancestors but they dressed themselves up in tartan and claimed to be just like the great Highland chiefs of the past.

In fact, few of these myth makers understood much about the real history of the Highlanders. However, they had a huge influence on what many people thought about the Highlands.

Real life there was very different.

— 14 —

Highland Life and Emigration

Most Highlanders were poor. They lived in small villages which had only four or five houses.

Around the houses the Highlanders grew their crops. The soil was neither deep nor fertile and there were problems with drainage so the Highlanders invented 'lazy beds'.

They dug deep ditches alongside the strips of land they wanted to cultivate. They piled all the earth from the ditches onto these strips. This increased the depth of soil they had. These ditches also improved drainage.

These strips were very narrow, and usually too steep for a horse drawn plough. The Highlanders turned the soil using a 'caschrom', which was a foot plough. They planted oats, barley and potatoes on these strips.

They also raised cattle on their common grazing which they sold to the Lowlanders in the autumn. They used the money they earned from these animals to pay rent to their landlord and to buy extra food.

Many Highlanders went to the Lowlands in the spring and autumn to work on farms there. This also earned them money.

Some went to the Lowlands and stayed there. Men found work in the new industries which were growing up. Women became servants either on farms or in the big houses of the Lowland gentry.

Emigration became popular in the Highlands at this time. Many of the young men had been soldiers and had served in the British Army in Canada and America. They realised that they could have a better standard of living if they left Scotland.

Many parts of the Highlands were affected by emigration. One or two young men would leave and then they would write home telling about how well they had prospered. That would encourage more people to go and, within a few years, whole villages would follow.

The home of the Duke of Argyll and one of his tenants.

The landowners were not pleased about this. They got no rent from empty villages and, besides, some of them had plans of their own. They hoped to build a canal through the Great Glen to link the west coast with the east. They planned to build factories there and, although the Highlanders did not know it, the chiefs planned to make them factory workers. These chiefs did everything they could to stop Highlanders leaving.

Some Highland chiefs turned their empty villages into sheep farms. New breeds of sheep, like the Cheviot and the Blackface were very profitable.

In fact, within a few years many chiefs realised that renting out sheep farms brought them bigger rents than letting people farm the land. They began to drive out the people to make more and bigger sheep farms. These evictions are known as the Highland Clearances.

This portrait is of the 4th Earl of Breadalbane. Burns addressed the poem to him.

From *ADDRESS OF BEELZEBUB*

In this poem Burns pretends to be the Devil (Beelzebub), encouraging Highland landlords to stop people emigrating from Glengarry to freedom in Canada.

Faith! you[1] and Applecross[2] were right
To keep the Highland hounds in sight!
I doubt na! they wad bid nae better[3]
Than let them ance[4] out owre[5] the water!
Then up amang thae[6] lakes and seas[7],
They'll mak what rules and laws they please...

They, an be damn'd! what right hae they
To meat or sleep, or light o day?
Far less to riches pow'r, or freedom,
But what your lordship likes to gie[8] them?

1 The Earl of Breadalbane who led this group of Highland landlords
2 another Highland landlord.
3 do any better
4 once
5 over
6 those
7 a reference to Canada
8 give

Influence of the Church

When Burns was alive Scotland was a very religious country. Most Lowland Scots were Protestants who attended the Church of Scotland regularly. In fact, in some places, people were fined if they did not attend all three church services on Sunday! People were also expected to hold religious services in their house every day.

Pupils in school were taught to read the Bible. They were also taught the catechism, which was a long list of questions and answers about the beliefs of the Church of Scotland. Everyone was expected to know the answers to these questions by heart. Ministers used to visit people's houses to make sure that everyone knew the catechism and to explain its meaning.

Ministers were helped in these duties by elders who were religious men elected by church-goers to help them. Each elder regularly visited a group of families to discuss the catechism and the minister's sermons.

The elders also kept an eye on people. They made sure that they attended the church regularly and that they lived religious lives and did not break any of the Ten Commandments.

They were particularly keen to find out why people missed church services and to catch anyone who worked on Sundays.

The Church, at that time, was very strict, but there were arguments about how strict it should be. One group, called the 'Auld Lights', was much stricter that the 'New Lights' and there were terrible arguments between the two groups. The Auld Lights, for example, did not approve of dancing and dance music and they wanted people to sing only religious music.

Of course, Robert Burns was aware of these arguments and, although he liked some people who were Auld Lights, he usually supported the New Lights.

He had a special dislike for people who claimed to be very religious but who, in fact, were not as good as they said. Robert Burns said that these people were hypocrites.

Ministers were very important men in the community. Most of them were gloomy figures, dressed in black from head to toe.

Burns was often in trouble with the Church. In particular he was very fond of 'the lassies' and he often fell in love – even although he was married to Jean Armour. Some of his best poems were written to ladies he loved.

Probably the most famous lady Burns courted was Mrs. Agnes (Nancy) McLehose. He met her when he visited Edinburgh and found out that her husband had left her and gone to live in Jamaica. Burns wrote many letters to her calling her by the secret name 'Clarinda'. In her replies to these letters Mrs McLehose called Burns 'Sylvander'.

Clarinda, Mrs. Agnes (Nancy) McLehose.

When Mrs McLehose left Scotland to join her husband in Jamaica, Burns wrote 'Ae Fond Kiss'. This became one of his most famous songs.

This is 'Holy Willie'. The poem Burns wrote about him pokes fun at hypocrites.

AE[1] FOND KISS

Ae fond kiss, and then we sever!
Ae fareweel, and then forever!
Deep in heart-wrung tears I'll pledge thee,
Warring sighs and groans I'll wage thee.

Who shall say that Fortune grieves him,
While the star of hope she leaves him?
Me, nae cheerfu twinkle lights me,
Dark despair around benights me.

I'll ne'er blame my partial fancy:
Naething[2] could resist my Nancy!
But to see her was to love her,
Love but her, and love forever.

Had we never lov'd sae[3] kindly,
Had we never lov'd sae blindly,
Never love - or never parted
We had ne'er been broken-hearted.

Fare-thee-weel[4], thou first and fairest!
Fare-thee-weel, thou best and dearest!
Thine be ilka[5] joy and treasure,
Peace, Enjoyment, Love, and Pleasure!

Ae fond kiss, and then we sever!
Ae farewell, alas, for ever!
Deep in heart-wrung tears I'll pledge thee
Warring sighs and groans I'll wage thee.

1 One
2 nothing
3 so
4 farewell
5 each or every

— 16 —

Poems and People

Robert Burns had the gift of using words in an amusing and clever way. He often wrote poems to compliment the women he met. Miss Deborah Davies was very small, so Burns wrote:

> *Ask why God made the gem so small,*
> *And why so huge the granite?*
> *Because God meant mankind should set*
> *That higher value on it.*

One Sunday, he sat beside Miss Rachel Ainslie while the minister preached a frightening sermon about how God punished wicked people. Burns took her Bible and wrote this verse on it.

> *Fair maid, you need not take the hint,*
> *Nor idle texts pursue;*
> *'Twas guilty sinners that he meant,*
> *Not angels such as you.*

These ladies were very pleased with their poems but not everyone was pleased with what Burns wrote. In the poem 'Willie Wastle', Burns describes Willie's wife.

> **She has an e'e[1] (she has but ane),**
> **The cat has twa the very colour,**
> **Five rusty teeth, forbye[2] a stump**
> **A clapper tongue wad deave[3] a miller;**
> **A whiskin beard about her mou[4],**
> **Her nose and chin they threaten ither**
> **Sic[5] a wife as Willie had,**
> **I wad na gie a button for her.**

1 eye
2 as well as
3 deafen
4 mouth
5 such

In 'Tam o' Shanter' Burns describes Tam o' Shanter's wife sitting at home waiting for him to come home from the pub.

> *Whare sits our sulky, sullen dame,*
> *Gathering her brows like gathering storm,*
> *Nursing her wrath to keep it warm.*

Sometimes, Burns made fun of the men he knew as well. One night, while drinking with friends, Burns saw a schoolteacher fall asleep in the corner. He made up the verse 'Epitaph for Willie Michie' about him. The schoolteacher might not have been pleased about this. Burns annoyed many people in this way.

Burns sometimes got into very serious trouble. Once, while he was visitig Stirling, he wrote a verse 'Written by Somebody on the Window', comparing the British Royal Family to the Stewart Kings of Scotland. King George III and his government would have been very annoyed about this verse. Indeed, sometimes it looked as if Burns was a Jacobite.

EPITAPH FOR WILLIAM MICHIE

Here lie Willie Michie's
  banes[1]:
O Satan, when ye tak him,
Gie him the schulin[2] o
  your weans[3],
For clever deils[4] he'll mak
  them!

1 bones
2 schooling
3 children
4 devils

WRITTEN BY SOMEBODY ON THE WINDOW

The injured Stewart line is gone,
A race outlandish fills their throne:
An idiot race, to honour lost
Who know them best despise them most.

George III,
drawn by a cartoonist
called James Gillray.

Poems and Politics

Burns was very lucky, in 1789, when the Government gave him a job as an exciseman in Dumfries. He had just moved to a new farm at Ellisland and, for the next three years, he tried to be a farmer and an exciseman. His job was to collect taxes from people who made or sold 'excisable goods' like beer, spirits, tobacco and even tea. Each week he had to travel many miles on horseback to do this. He also had to stop smugglers who tried to bring these items into the country without paying taxes.

This could be dangerous work. There could be a fight if the smugglers wanted to escape. Once, Robert Burns and a group of excisemen had to wade into the sea to catch some smugglers by surprise.

Because he worked for the Government, Burns needed to be very careful about what he wrote. However, he still wrote some poems which upset his employers and the rich people in Britain.

In 1789 there was a revolution in France. The King lost his power over the country and the French people said that everyone in France was to be equal. They banned all noble titles and took away all the special rights and powers that nobles had over ordinary men and women.

This idea excited Burns. Like the French, he agreed that an honest person was as good as any nobleman, and better than a dishonest or a stupid noble. He said so in his poem 'A Man's a Man'. Many British people agreed with him. The British nobles, however, still had a great deal of power. They were very displeased about what he wrote. They were worried about a revolution happening in Britain.

Unfortunately for Burns, the French Revolution became very violent. The French beheaded the King of France and they began to kill all the noblemen and priests. France became a very violent country and, during the 'Reign of Terror', the French killed anyone who complained about their Revolutionary Government.

In his poem 'A Man's a Man' Burns wrote:

A prince can mak a belted knight[1],
A marquis, duke, an a' that!
But an honest man's aboon[2] his might –
Guid faith he mauna fa' that[3]!
For a' that, an a' that,
Their dignities, an a' that,
The pith o sense[4] an pride o worth[5],
Are higher rank than a' that.

1 nobleman
2 above
3 Good faith! He cannot find fault with that.
4 strong common sense
5 self-confidence

In Britain, the King and his Government decided to punish British supporters of the French Revolution. Lord Braxfield sent Thomas Muir to a prison colony in Australia for supporting revolutionary ideas in Scotland. Burns found himself in trouble again. He was very worried that he would be sacked or put in prison. He became much more careful about what he wrote.

Britain finally went to war against France in 1793 to stop a revolution. The French then threatened to invade Britain. All over the country men joined local regiments, called militia, and trained to fight any invaders who landed in their area. In Dumfries-shire, the men formed the Dumfries Volunteers. Burns decided to join it and, in his spare time, he trained to be a soldier. He had to pay for his own uniform, which was very expensive, and he even had to buy his own weapons.

He also began to write poems against the French and their ideas, and in support of the British King and his Government.

Burns in the uniform of the Dumfries Volunteers.

From DOES HAUGHTY[1] GAUL[2] INVASION THREAT?

Does haughty Gaul invasion threat?
Then let the loons[3] beware, Sir!
There's wooden walls[4] upon our seas
And volunteers[5] on shore, Sir!....

The wretch that would a tyrant[6] own
And the wretch, his true-sworn brother,
Who would set the mob above the throne,
May they be damn'd together!
Who will not sing God Save the King
Shall hang as high 's the steeple;
But while we sing God save the King
We'll ne'er forget the people!

1 proud   4 the Royal Navy
2 France   5 part-time soldiers
3 fools   6 cruel ruler

— 18 —

Medicine

Between 1750 and 1800, nine out of ten of all the doctors who qualified in Britain were trained in Scotland. The country's medical schools, particularly Edinburgh's, had good reputations and attracted students from abroad.

In Scotland, doctors were prepared to think about the health of the whole population, and not just of a few rich patients. This was important in Scotland's growing towns where people were often crowded into poor housing and dirty conditions.

Diseases like smallpox, typhus, diphtheria, tuberculosis and cholera were common. Many children died. In fact, only three of the nine children of Robert Burns and Jean Armour grew up to be adults. By the end of the century, however, people were using a vaccine to prevent smallpox, which had often killed large numbers of children.

Medicine was beginning to become more scientific but there were no anaesthetics or antiseptics. This meant that patients were wide awake during operations, and many died from shock or from wound infections.

To reduce the pain and shock to patients, surgeons tried to work very quickly. They needed to understand the anatomy (parts) of the body very well. So, they practised cutting up dead bodies.

Only the bodies of condemned criminals were available, so there was always a shortage of corpses. This led to a gruesome trade in corpses, as grave robbers stole bodies and sold them to the anatomists.

This army medical kit shows the instruments doctors used when Burns was alive.

DEATH AND DOCTOR HORNBOOK

Whare I kill'd ane, a fair strae death[1]
By loss o blood or want o breath,
This night I'm free to tak my aith[2]
That Hornbook's skill
Has clad a score i their last claith[3]
By drap an pill.

An honest wabster[4] to his trade,
Whase wife's twa nieves[5] were scarce
* weel-bred*
Gat tippence worth to mend her head,
When it was sair;
The wife slade cannie[6] to her bed
But ne'er spak mair.

That's just a swatch[7] o Hornbook's way;
Thus goes he on from day to day,
Thus does he poison, kill, an slay
An's weel paid for't;
Yet stop me o my lawfu prey,
Wi his damn'd dirt.

1 death in bed	5 fists
2 oath	6 crept quietly
3 cloth	7 sample
4 weaver	

This picture shows death looking on as the chemist mixes Dr Hornbook's prescription.

In a letter to a friend, Gilbert Burns, the poet's brother, described how Robert's ill-health began when he was working at Mount Oliphant.

Gilbert believed that the hard work and sorrow Robert endured there was largely to blame for his frequent problems.

There were few reliable medicines. A list in a medical book published in Edinburgh in 1737 included the juice of woodlice, crushed toad and spiders' webs! In some cases, people used herbal remedies which did some good.

In his poem 'Death and Doctor Hornbook' Burns poked fun at a schoolteacher who was trying a bit of doctoring using just a medical book. In it, the poet pretended to talk with Death who complained about Hornbook and his so-called cures. Death was fed up because Hornbook's 'cures' were killing people faster than he could.

Burns was often worried by his serious ill-health. Rheumatic fever in his youth, when he did very heavy work on a poor diet, had left him with a damaged heart. Like many people in his time, he needed better medical help than was available to him.

'At this time he was almost always troubled in the evenings by a dull headache, which, at a future period of his life, turned into a rapid beating of the heart, and a threatening of fainting and suffocation in his bed, in the night time.'

SCOTLAND
in the time of
BURNS

— 19 —

The Burns Legacy

In 1791, Burns gave up his farm at Ellisland and moved into the town of Dumfries to concentrate on his work as an exciseman. The quality and quantity of his writing at this time, particularly his songs, show that his great creative talent was as strong as ever.

However, his damaged heart was growing weaker and he died on the 21 July 1796. He was only thirty-seven years old.

Since his death, statues and memorials have been built all over the world as signs of the deep admiration people have felt for Burns and his work.

Over the years, however, the Scots language Burns used has continued to decline and our way of life has changed greatly.

For these reasons, many Scots now need to look up a glossary to find out the meanings of some words he used.

Readers all over the English-speaking world have to do the same and find it is worth the effort. They discover that Burns's views and thoughts are close to their own. They share his feelings about snobbery, injustice, love and friendship.

This is why Burns is a world poet. His poems and songs have been translated into many languages including Japanese, Chinese and Russian.

The song 'Auld Lang Syne' is a world anthem for friendship.

from AULD LANG SYNE[1]

Verse
Should auld acquaintance[2] be forgot,
And never brought to mind? Should auld
acquaintance be forgot,
And auld lang syne?

Chorus
For auld lang syne, my dear,
For auld lang syne,
We'll tak a cup o kindness yet,
For auld lang syne!

Verse
And there's a hand my trusty fiere[3],
And gie's a hand o thine, And we'll tak a
right guid-willie waught[4]
For auld lang syne.

1 old long ago (old times)
2 friendship
3 friend
4 goodwill drink

Perhaps the spirit in which Burns is best remembered is shown in those poems and songs that simply wish for fairness, and peace between people.

This engraving is of the statue of Burns at Dumfries.

from A MAN'S A MAN FOR A' THAT

Then let us pray that come it may
(As come it will for a' that),
That Sense and Worth oe'r a' the earth,
Shall bear the gree[1] an a' that.
For a' that and a' that,
It's comin yet for a' that,
That man to man, the world o'er
Shall brithers be for a' that.

1 be most important or take first place

People stand in a circle and hold hands while they sing the first verse and chorus of 'Auld Lang Syne'. At the start of the second verse they cross their arms to shake each others' hands while they are singing.

The Land of Burns

The map opposite shows some of the places associated with Robert Burns. In many places there are museums and visitor centres where you can find out more about the poet and his life and times.

In 1759 Burns was born on 25 January in a 'clay biggin' in **Alloway**.

In 1766 his family moved to **Mount Oliphant Farm**.

In 1777, when Robert was eighteen, they moved to **Lochlea Farm**.

In 1781 Burns moved to **Irvine** for almost a year to learn about the flax trade.

In 1782 he returned to **Lochlea** farm.

In 1784 Robert's father died. Robert and his brother rented the farm of **Mossgeil**, two miles from Lochlea, and took the family there.

In 1786 Burns visited **Edinburgh** for the first time

In 1788 Burns married Jean Armour and moved to **Ellisland Farm**.

In 1791 Robert Burns moved, with his wife and family, to **Dumfries** where he worked as an exciseman.

In 1793 the family moved to the house in **Bank Street, Dumfries** (now renamed Burns Street) where the poet died in 1796.

Places to visit

1 The cottage where Burns was born, now part of the Burns National Heritage Park

2 The Auld Kirk where the witches danced in Burn's poem, and the nearby *Tam o' Shanter* Experience visitor centre

3 The Glasgow Vennel in Irvine, where Burns went to learn about the flax business, is open to the public.

4 The Burns Museum in Wellwood, Irvine. Wellwood is also the home of the Irvine Burns Club.

5 Burns House Museum, Mauchline.

6 The Bachelors Club, Tarbolton, where Burns attended dancing classes, is open to the public.

7 Ellisland Farm in Dumfries is open to the public.

8 Burns House in Dumfries, where the poet died in 1796, is now a museum.

9 The Burns Mausoleum in Dumfries, where Burns is buried.

10 The Robert Burns Centre, Dumfries.

11 The Writers Museum, Edinburgh, has a display dedicated to Burns.